COURTNEY CRUMRIN IN THE TWILIGHT KINGDOM™

for Julie and for Corinne

COURTNEY CRUMRIN IN THE TWILIGHT KINGDOM™

By Ted Naifeh

Design by
Ted Naifeh
with assistance from Steven Birch @ Servo

Edited by
Joe Nozemack & James Lucas Jones

Published by Oni Press, Inc.
Joe Nozemack, publisher
James Lucas Jones, senior editor
Randal C. Jarrell, managing editor
Ian Shaughnessy, editorial assistant

This collects issues 1-4 of the Oni Press
comics series *Courtney Crumrin in the Twilight Kingdom*.

ONI PRESS, INC.
6336 SE Milwaukie Avenue, PMB 30
Portland, OR 97202
USA

www.onipress.com
www.tednaifeh.com

First edition: September 2004
ISBN 1-932664-01-7

1 3 5 7 9 10 8 6 4 2
PRINTED IN CANADA.

THERE GOES LI'L MISS COURTNEY CRUMRIN, OFF ON ANOTHER ADVENTURE...

BRINGIN' *HORROR* N' *GRIEF* TEH INNOCENT FOLK *EVERYWHERE*. HAR HAR!

YEH THINK OL' BUTTERWORM'S *EXAGGERATIN*'?

WELL, 'ER *LAST* ADVENTURE LEFT THE WHOLE COVEN O' MYSTICS IN TURMOIL...

...AND THE COVEN MARSHAL A MIDNIGHT *SNACK* FOR OL' TOMMY RAWHEAD, THE *HOBGOBLIN* WHAT LIVES IN THE MARLPIT.

NOT TEH *MENTION* BREAKIN' HER POOR OLD UNCLE ALOYSIUS'S *HEART*.

OH, SHE'S A *NASTY* PIECE O' WORK, RIGHT ENOUGH.

AN' IT LOOKS LIKE I AIN'T THE *ONLY* ONE THINKS SO.

CHAPTER ONE

I SEE. COMES BACK TO VISIT, DOES HE?

WELL, NOT YET, SO FAR AS I KNOW.

BUT YOU NEVER KNOW.

I SUPPOSE NOT.

For Sale
Grubb and Grubb
Real Estate

WHAT'S IT LIKE LIVING WITH THAT WEIRD UNCLE GUY?

EH, HE'S NOT SO BAD.

HOW'S LIFE IN THE HOOD THESE DAYS?

OH, YOU KNOW, MUCH BETTER SINCE YOU LEFT.

BUTTFACE.

DAD WORKS ALL THE TIME NOW.

I DON'T LIKE IT AT HOME ANYMORE.

YOU NEVER DID WITH YOUR MOM THE WAY SHE WAS.

IT'S WORSE NOW.

YEAH.

'SUP, DUDE.

HEY, DOGG. WHAT'S THE HAPS, YO?

COURTNEY WASN'T REALLY AT ALL SURPRISED TO SEE PETE AND TROY.

OH, HEY, GUYS. WASSUP?

THEY WERE FIXTURES, THE KIND OF GUYS WHO WERE DESTINED TO HANG OUT ON THE SAME STREET CORNER THEIR WHOLE LIVES.

THEY WEREN'T EXACTLY SWORN ENEMIES, BUT COURTNEY DIDN'T HAVE ANY WARM FUZZY FEELINGS FOR THEM EITHER.

NOTHIN', MAN.

JUST HANGIN'.

'SUP?

HEY, GUYS. LONG TIME.

CRUMRIN. HEARD YOU GOT RICH.

YEAH, LOADED. MY LIMO'S WAITING AROUND THE CORNER.

THREE!

TWO!

AND SHE'D GOTTEN GOOD AT WINNING, WITH OR WITHOUT ALLIES.

SHE WASN'T PARTICULARLY UPSET ABOUT THE GAME.

SHE THOUGHT SHE UNDERSTOOD THE RULES NOW.

GAAAHH!!!

Thubbb!

BAD LUCK.

LOOKS LIKE I'M NOT THE ONLY ONE TRIPPIN', YO.

THINGS DIDN'T GO WELL AFTER THAT, THOUGH COURTNEY AND MALCOLM DID WIN SIX GAMES IN A ROW. TROY WAS A REAL MESS BY THE END OF THE DAY.

I DON'T *REALLY* CARE *WHAT* THEY THINK OF ME. THEY'RE *JERKS.*

DUDE! THEY'RE MY *FRIENDS.*

DON'T BE TALKIN' SMACK ABOUT MY FRIENDS.

YOU USED TO TALK SMACK ABOUT 'EM *PLENTY,* FROM WHAT *I* REMEMBER.

CAN'T YOU DO *BETTER* THAN *TWEEDLE DEE* AND *TWEEDLE DUMBASS?*

SORRY! I DON'T HAVE A BUNCH OF *RICH BRATS* TO SPONGE OFF.

AT LEAST I CAN DEPEND ON THEM.

HE HADN'T SAID, *"UNLIKE YOU,"* BUT COURTNEY HEARD IT ANYWAY.

COURTNEY HAD UNCLE ALOYSIUS, SUCH AS HE WAS, AND EVEN MS. CRISP, WHEN SHE WASN'T BEING AN OVERBEARING TYRANT.

ALL MALCOLM HAD WAS A BIG EMPTY HOUSE, TWEEDLE DEE, AND TWEEDLE DUMBASS.

IT WAS PERHAPS THE FIRST TIME IN HER LIFE THAT COURTNEY FELT WORSE FOR SOMEONE ELSE THAN FOR HERSELF.

HOW GOES THE SALE, POP?

HMM?

OH. FINE, JUST FINE.

I'M REELING THEM IN, HONEY.

IT'S JUST THAT THE AD DIDN'T MENTION IT WAS A FIXER-UPPER.

OH, I WOULDN'T SAY FIXER-UPPER.

A LITTLE PAINT AND POLISH SHOULD TAKE CARE OF IT.

UH-HUH.

SHOULD I JUST PUT THIS BACK, OR DO YOU WANT TO POLISH IT FIRST?

JUST REELING 'EM IN.

COURTNEY NEVER USED TO WALK THESE STREETS AT NIGHT.

IT WASN'T THAT IT WAS A "BAD" NEIGHBORHOOD, BUT LITTLE GIRLS NEED TO BE CAREFUL.

OF COURSE THESE DAYS, THE NIGHT HELD NO TERROR FOR COURTNEY CRUMRIN.

QUIET!

WHO'S THAT?

IN HILLSBOROUGH, SHE WAS THE ONE THE OTHER KIDS DIDN'T WANT TO RUN INTO IN THE DARK.

DUNNO. LET'S BAIL, DUDE.

NO MATTER HOW BAD THEY WERE, SHE COULD BE WORSE.

BUT IT WAS COLD COMFORT, BEING THE SCARIEST THING IN THE NEIGHBORHOOD.

HEY, BUTTFACE.

SORRY ABOUT LAST NIGHT.

IT'S COOL. I WAS BEING A JERK.

IT'S JUST... THINGS ARE DIFFERENT NOW. PETE AND TROY, YA KNOW, THEY AREN'T SO BAD.

I KNOW THEY USED TO BE MORONS.

HEY, IT'S NONE OF MY BUSINESS.

JUST... BE COOL.

DON'T DO ANYTHING STUPID.

Papa Giordano's TRATTORIA Est. 1962

WHAT'S THAT SUPPOSED TO MEAN?

YA KNOW, DON'T GET YOURSELF INTO TROUBLE.

RIPPING OFF BIKES, THAT KIND OF THING.

AS COURTNEY WATCHED THEM GO, SHE TOLD HERSELF ALL SORTS OF THINGS...

IT WAS NONE OF HER BUSINESS.

GOT A *NEW* BIKE, DUDE.

YOU CAN HAVE *THAT* ONE.

YOU COULDN'T MAKE PEOPLE CHANGE.

WHO WAS SHE TO JUDGE, ANYWAY?

LET HIM GO.

THE FURTHER SHE FOLLOWED THEM, THE FEEBLER HER ARGUMENTS BECAME.

I DON'T *KNOW*, MAN, IT'S JUST A *FEELIN'*.

SHE WAS GIVING US THE EVIL EYE. SHE'S *BAD LUCK*.

AIN'T NOTHIN' PERSONAL, BUT I DON'T LIKE YOU HANGIN' WITH HER.

SHE'S MY FRIEND, DUDE. DON'T BE ALL LIKE THAT.

YOU USED TO BE FRIENDS, MAN. JUST 'CAUSE SHE SHOWS UP FOR A FEW DAYS DOESN'T MEAN NOTHIN'.

YEAH. MAYBE.

I'M YOUR FRIEND, MAN. AND I'M TELLING YOU, I KNOW A NARC WHEN I SEE ONE. IF SHE KNEW WHAT WE WERE DOIN' RIGHT NOW...

...WE'D SEE WHAT KIND OF FRIEND SHE REALLY WAS.

DUDE, CHECK THIS OUT!

AWESOME! WHERE'D YOU FIND THAT?

THIS WAY.

THERE'S ALL KINDS O' STUFF.

FREEZE!!!

DON'T EVEN *THINK* ABOUT IT, MISTER!

DON'T STOP, DUDE.

I SAID FREEZE!

HOW'D YOU DO THAT? YOU *PULLED* US RIGHT THROUGH THE *GLASS*.

I'VE LEARNED A FEW TRICKS *MYSELF* OVER THE LAST YEAR.

BANG!

OH NO!

OH, HI, SWEETY.

DIDN'T HEAR YOU COME IN. HAVE A NICE DAY?

COURTNEY FOUND HER FATHER LOOKING AS EXHAUSTED AS SHE FELT.

HEY, POP.

HIS COLLECTION OF BILLS, DEBTS, AND EXPENSES HAD GROWN SINCE THE DAY BEFORE, AND NOW COVERED THE LITTLE TABLE.

BY THE LOOK OF THINGS, MR. CRUMRIN WAS UP TO HIS EARS IN REALITY. HE DIDN'T NEED ANYMORE.

FINE.

THAT'S GOOD.

SOMETIMES I THINK WE HAVEN'T BEEN TAKING GOOD CARE OF YOU, HONEY.

I THINK ABOUT ALL THE THINGS I'D PROMISED MYSELF I'D GIVE YOU.

WHAT DO YOU MEAN?

YOU KNOW, A BIG HOUSE. PRETTY CLOTHES.

I'D ALWAYS WANTED TO GET YOU A NICE CAR WHEN YOU WERE OLD ENOUGH.

WE'VE TRIED TO BE GOOD PARENTS, BUT SOMETIMES I LOOK AT YOU AND WONDER, "WHAT'S WRONG? WHAT AREN'T WE GIVING YOU?"

I DON'T KNOW, POP.

I DON'T REALLY NEED ANYTHING.

I REALLY DO.

HE GAZED SADLY AT THE LITTLE MOUND OF PAPERS BEFORE HIM, AS THOUGH TRYING TO FIND A PIECE OF A PUZZLE THAT JUST WASN'T THERE.

YES, YOU DO.

AND I *WISH* I COULD GIVE IT TO YOU.

C'MON, MALCOLM. OPEN UP.

COURTNEY KNEW THERE WAS NOTHING SHE COULD DO TO SALVAGE HER FRIENDSHIP WITH MALCOLM.

SHE WASN'T SURE SHE EVEN LIKED HIM ANYMORE.

BUT SHE DID KNOW THAT SHE WANTED THE LAST WORD.

MALCOLM?

HE'S NOT HERE.

YEAH, SURE.

OH... HEY, MRS. BIGGS.

IT'S COURTNEY, ISN'T IT?

SORRY, HON, MY MIND AIN'T WHAT IT *USED* TO BE.

SMALL WONDER.

MALCOLM DOESN'T SPEND MUCH TIME AT *HOME* THESE DAYS.

IF YOU SEE HIM, TELL HIM HIS *MOMMA MISSES* HIM.

COURTNEY FELT A CHILL OF APPREHENSION AS SHE MET THE OLDER WOMAN'S GAZE.

SOMETHING CHILLY IN THOSE EYES BROUGHT A PANG OF GURGLING FEAR DEEP IN HER GUT.

NOW NO OFFENCE, BUT YOU GOT TO GO, CHILD.

TO BE *HONEST*, I'VE NEVER REALLY *LIKED* YOU.

BUT COURTNEY HAD FACED WORSE.

I *KNOW* YOU DIDN'T. I'M NOT *EXACTLY* A BRIGHT RAY OF SUNSHINE.

BUT *I* ALWAYS LIKED *YOU.*

I ALWAYS WISHED MY MOM CARED ABOUT *ME* AS MUCH AS *YOU* CARE ABOUT *MALCOLM.*

HE'S *MY* BOY. I TAKE *GOOD CARE* OF HIM...

I *KNOW.*

BUT *I* THINK YOU'VE HUNG AROUND HERE LONG ENOUGH.

EXCUSE ME?

YOU'RE WONDERING WHY MALCOLM DOESN'T COME HOME?

WHY MR. B IS WORKING ALL THE TIME?

YOU'VE GOT SOME NERVE TALKING TO ME LIKE THAT IN MY OWN HOME.

LOOK, MRS. B. I KNOW YOU MEAN WELL, BUT YOU AREN'T DOING MALCOLM ANY GOOD ANYMORE.

YOU'RE JUST MESSING HIM UP. IT'S TIME TO CUT THE CORD.

WHO'RE YOU TO TELL ME WHAT'S GOOD FOR MY SON?

I'M HIS FRIEND. I MAY NOT BE MUCH OF A FRIEND, BUT I KNOW WHAT'S GOOD FOR HIM, AND THAT AIN'T YOU.

NOW GET GOING, BEFORE I GET MEAN.

COURTNEY FOUND HER PARENTS IN A SURPRISINGLY GOOD MOOD.

WHAT'S GOING ON?

COURTNEY, THIS IS MR. AND MRS. JONES.

THEY'VE JUST BOUGHT OUR *HOUSE*!

HELLO, YOUNG LADY.

WHAT A CHARMING... UH... BARRETTE.

IT'S JUST A PHASE.

KIDS, HUH?

UM... YEAH.

THAT WAS THE LAST TIME COURTNEY EVER SAW THE HOUSE SHE'D GROWN UP IN, AND THE FIRST TIME SHE'D FOUND HERSELF LOOKING FORWARD TO LEAVING IT, AND GOING TO HER NEW HOME.

OH, THANK GOODNESS WE CAN GET RID OF THIS *JUNKER* AND GET THAT SUV.

SO, HONEY, YOUR BIRTHDAY IS COMING UP. WHO'S UP FOR A *SHOPPING SPREE*!?!

...GRUMBLE...

CHAPTER TWO

YOU *KNOW* I CAN'T AFFORD TO BE SEEN WITH YOU THESE DAYS.

I JUST WANTED TO TALK ABOUT *COURTNEY.*

WHAT *ABOUT* HER?

YOU KNOW *EXACTLY* WHAT I'M TALKING ABOUT. SOONER OR LATER YOU'RE GOING TO HAVE TO FACE YOUR *RESPONSIBILITIES...*

WHETHER YOU *WANT* TO OR *NOT.*

PERHAPS.

COURTNEY HAD RESISTED, BUT THERE'S JUST NO ARGUING WITH MS. CRISP. APPARENTLY, MANY LOCAL FAMILIES SENT THEIR CHILDREN TO SATURDAY SCHOOL AT RADLEY HALL, PARTLY TO LEARN COVEN HISTORY, BUT MOSTLY TO MEET OTHER CHILDREN OF WITCHES AND WARLOCKS.

IT SUPPOSEDLY DID THEM GOOD TO MEET KIDS LIKE THEMSELVES, FROM WHOM THEY NEED KEEP NO SECRETS.

SERENITY CARTER AND URSULA WILSON HAD SETTLED IN HILLSBOROUGH WITH THEIR HUSBANDS WHEN IT WAS STILL WILD COUNTRY.

THAT WAS THE FIRST COUNCIL.

THE COVEN ITSELF WAS FOUNDED EIGHTY YEARS EARLIER BY THREE IMMIGRANT WOMEN.

THEY'D FOUND OLD RAVANNA ALREADY LIVING THERE, ON THE LAND OF A RETIRED ARMY COLONEL NAMED CRUMRIN.

AS THE WILDERNESS SLOWLY BECAME A VILLAGE, THE THREE WOMEN BECAME FRIENDS. RAVANNA TAUGHT THE OTHERS THE SECRETS OF WITCHCRAFT.

THIS SPECIAL KNOWLEDGE IS PROBABLY WHAT HELPED BOTH FAMILIES ACHIEVE PROSPERITY.

SERENITY AND URSULA TAUGHT THEIR CHILDREN THE SECRETS THEY'D LEARNED, AND SOON THERE WERE PRACTICING WITCHES AND WARLOCKS ALL OVER THE COUNTRYSIDE.

RAVANNA NEVER MARRIED, BUT IT WAS RUMORED THAT SHE BORE COLONEL CRUMRIN A SON, WHOM SHE TAUGHT HER GREATEST SECRETS.

IN ANY EVENT, THOUGH HE WAS A LIFELONG BACHELOR, COLONEL CRUMRIN LEFT HIS LAND TO A YOUNG MAN NAMED NICHOLAS, WHO ALSO SEEMED TO HAVE AN UNCANNY PENCHANT FOR PROSPERITY.

THE WITCHES AND WARLOCKS, WHO BY NOW FORMED A LARGE COMMUNITY, ALWAYS DEFERRED TO THE THREE FOUNDING WOMEN.

WHEN AT LAST OLD RAVANNA DIED (SHE'D OUTLIVED THE OTHERS BY ALMOST TWENTY YEARS), FOLKS FELT THEY NEEDED NEW LEADERSHIP, OF A MORE OFFICIAL SORT.

AND THAT'S WHEN THE COUNCIL WAS FORMED.

ANY QUESTIONS?

WHO'S MR. MANDRAKE?

THE OLD TEACHER. THEY SAY HE WAS THE GREATEST WARLOCK LIVING.

WELL, HE SAID IT, ANYWAY.

I THOUGHT HE WAS A TWIT. THAT BIG HAIR. HE LOOKED LIKE A GIRL.

AND I NEVER SAW HIM DO ANYTHING, YOU KNOW... MAGICAL.

HORRIBLE WAY TO GO THOUGH.

EATEN BY A HOBGOBLIN.

WHERE'D YOU HEAR THAT ANYWAY?

HE WAS TEASING YOU, CHAS. PEOPLE DON'T GET EATEN BY GOBLINS ANYMORE.

MY BROTHER.

>SNORT<

WHO'S THAT?

SHE'S NEW, TOO. I THINK HER NAME'S CRUMRIN.

COURTNEY CRUMRIN.

OH.

SOMETHING I CAN DO FOR YOU, DEPUTY?

OH...

EXCUSE MY *INTRUSION*, MS. CRISP.

I WAS HOPING TO, UM, ASK YOU SOME QUESTIONS.

REGARDING?

ONE OF YOUR *STUDENTS*. MISS CRUMRIN.

WHAT ABOUT HER?

BRIGHT GIRL, IS SHE?

I'D SAY SO..

EXCEPTIONALLY BRIGHT?

MAYBE. MORE THAN USUALLY *CURIOUS*, ANYWAY. WHAT'S THIS ABOUT?

I *CAN'T* SAY AT THE MOMENT.

I'M JUST A BIT CURIOUS ABOUT HER.

COURTNEY HAD NEVER FELT SO LONELY.

SHE HADN'T EXCHANGED SO MUCH AS A WORD WITH UNCLE ALOYSIUS IN WEEKS.

SHE'D RECENTLY LEARNED FROM MS. CRISP THAT HE WAS TO GO AWAY FOR THE WHOLE SUMMER.

AS THE DAYS PASSED BY WITH NO ONE TO TALK TO, SHE FELT AS THOUGH SOMETHING WAS SLIPPING IRRETRIEVABLY FROM HER GRASP, AND SHE WAS POWERLESS TO STOP IT.

I KNOW ALL KINDS OF SPELLS. I CAN MAKE A *COW* STOP GIVING MILK.

ONLY WE DON'T *HAVE* A COW.

THAT'S HANDY.

I CAN TELL *FORTUNES.* I LEARNED FROM MY GRANDPA.

WOW. MY MOM'S TEACHING ME THAT. DO YOU USE *TAROT CARDS* OR READ *TEA LEAVES?*

I, UM, I READ *HANDKERCHIEFS.*

HANDKERCHIEFS?

YEAH. YOU BLOW YOUR *NOSE—*

OKAY, STOP!

YOU DON'T NEED TO PAINT A *PICTURE.*

THOSE ARE THE *LAMEST* SPELLS I'VE EVER HEARD.

I KNOW A *LOVE SPELL.* MY *MOM* TAUGHT ME. IT CAN MAKE SOMEONE *LOVE* YOU TILL THEY *DIE.*

WOW! HAVE YOU EVER *DONE IT?*

YOU HAVE TO DO IT AT *MIDNIGHT,* AND MY BEDTIME'S *NINE.*

LAME!

OKAY, MR. *WITCHIER-THAN-THOU.* WHAT CAN *YOU* DO?

IT JUST SO *HAPPENS* I DO KNOW A LITTLE SPELL.

YEAH, WHAT'S IT *DO?* MAKE YOUR *EYEBROWS* GROW TOGETHER?

ONLY ONE WAY TO *FIND OUT.*

SORRY TO *KEEP* YOU, COUNCILORS. I'M AFRAID YOUR *SUMMONS* CAUGHT ME BY *SURPRISE.*

MM HMM. HAVE A *SEAT,* DEPUTY.

YES, SIR. MAY I ASK WHAT THIS IS REGARDING?

TEMPLETON, SOMETHING HAS COME TO OUR ATTENTION THAT, FRANKLY, WE FIND DISTURBING.

INDEED?

NOW *CLEARLY* WE DON'T HAVE THE WHOLE *STORY*, SO I JUST WANTED TO GET IT FROM YOU *PERSONALLY.*

WHAT *EXACTLY* IS YOUR INTEREST IN YOUNG MISS *CRUMRIN?*

SIR? UH... WHY DO YOU ASK?

PERHAPS WE'RE *OVER-REACTING,* BUT–

LET'S NOT MINCE *WORDS,* DEPUTY.

WE CAME ACROSS CERTAIN THINGS IN YOUR *OFFICE* THAT I THINK YOU'D BETTER *EXPLAIN.*

EXCUSE ME, SIRS. I'M NOT SURE IT'S *APPROPRIATE* FOR YOU TO BE RIFLING THROUGH MY FILES.

GIVEN RECENT *EVENTS,* YOU'LL HAVE TO PARDON OUR CURIOSITY.

THAT IS AN INTERESTING LOOKING SPELL.

YEAH. COOL, HUH?

DO YOU KNOW WHAT IT DOES?

OF COURSE. IT TURNS THE VICT— THE, UH, SUBJECT INTO A NIGHT THING.

WOW!

COOL!

WHAT!?!

PRETTY NEAT. SO YOU KNOW HOW TO UNDO IT?

NOW LEAVE THE KID *ALONE*, OR I'LL *GIVE* YOU SOMETHING TO CURSE ABOUT.

WHO MADE YOU COVEN MARSHALL, ANYWAY?

YEAH, WHO DO YOU THINK YOU *ARE*?

I'M *JUST* PROTECTING...

JOEY.

JOEY. YEAH.

I DON'T *NEED* YOUR PROTECTION. BLAKE'S MY *BROTHER*, HE WOULDN'T DO ANYTHING TO HURT ME.

COURTNEY LOOKED OVER THE DISTRUSTFUL FACES OF THE OTHER CHILDREN AND REALIZED THAT MOUNTAIN RANGES OF STUPIDITY STOOD BETWEEN THEM.

BLAKE OBVIOUSLY COULDN'T MAGIC HIS WAY OUT OF A PAPER BAG.

HOW HAD HE BEATEN HER?

HER ANGER WAS DWARFED BY THE HUMILIATION OF BEING OSTRACIZED ONCE AGAIN. HER ONLY COMFORT WAS THE BITTER KNOWLEDGE THAT WHATEVER TROUBLE THEY GOT INTO WAS WELL DESERVED.

OKAY, LET'S DO THIS THING.

LISTEN TO ME, TEMPLETON.

YOU'VE GOT TO SEE HOW *INSANE* THIS SOUNDS.

AND MY EVIDENCE COUNTS FOR *NOTHING?* THIS "CHILD," AS YOU CALL HER, HAS LEFT A TRAIL OF *TERROR.*

I'VE INTERVIEWED CHILDREN FROM HER *SCHOOL—*

YES, AND THEY'VE ALL NOTICED HOW ODD SHE IS.

SHE'S A *CRUMRIN*, TEMPLETON.

ALOYSIUS IS THE SAME WAY. WE'VE HAD TO *SPEAK* TO HIM ABOUT THE ATTENTION HE ATTRACTS.

BUT IF *ECCENTRICITY* WERE A CRIME, WE'D *ALL* BE LOCKED UP.

ECCENTRIC IS ONE THING. BUT I HAVE REASON TO SUSPECT THAT THE GIRL WAS INVOLVED IN HECTOR'S MURDER.

WE DON'T *KNOW* WHAT BECAME OF HECTOR.

ANYHOW, YOU SAW HIS *CELLAR.* YOU KNOW WHAT KIND OF MAN HE *REALLY* WAS.

I...

I HAVE TROUBLE *BELIEVING* EVERYTHING I SAW DOWN THERE.

I WORKED *CLOSELY* WITH HIM FOR YEARS.

I HAVE REASON TO SUSPECT...

GENTLEMEN.

MADAM.

...COUNCILOR.

SUSPECT *WHAT?*

...THAT THERE ARE PEOPLE WHO WOULD GO TO *ANY* LENGTHS TO *COVER* FOR HER.

HER *UNCLE,* FOR STARTERS.

TEMPLETON, I'M YOUR *FATHER,* AND I'M *TELLING* YOU THAT IF YOU PURSUE THIS *FURTHER,* YOU MAY *RUIN* YOUR CAREER.

WE'VE BROUGHT *ENOUGH* UNDUE GRIEF TO THAT FAMILY.

I *DON'T* CARE TO BRING ANY *MORE.*

COURTNEY DIDN'T UNDERSTAND WHY THIS LATEST REJECTION WAS SO UPSETTING.

THESE COVEN CHILDREN WERE EVERY BIT AS HEARTLESS AND FOOLISH AS ALL THE OTHER KIDS OF HILLSBOROUGH.

BUT THEIR RECKLESS CURIOSITY ABOUT WITCHCRAFT SEEMED ALL TOO FAMILIAR.

SEEING THE WICKED GLEAM IN BLAKE'S EYE...

...WAS LIKE LOOKING INTO A MIRROR.

COURTNEY WAS UNSURPRISED TO SEE JOEY ABSENT THE NEXT WEEK.

WELL, I HOPE HE FEELS BETTER SOON, BLAKE.

BUT I'LL BE EXPECTING YOU TO BRING HIM HIS HOMEWORK.

SHE THOUGHT SHE COULD GUESS WHAT BLAKE'S EXPRESSION MEANT.

YES, MS. CRISP.

WHAT STUNG MOST WAS THE KNOWLEDGE THAT HER OWN MISERY WAS PERHAPS NO LESS DESERVED THAN THEIRS. IT'S A HARSH LESSON TO FIND YOURSELF ON THE SAME SCALES OF MERIT BY WHICH YOU MEASURE OTHERS.

AFTER ALL, WHATEVER THEY'D MANAGED, SHE'D DONE WORSE. THAT SHE'D DONE IT TO THE DESERVING WAS SMALL COMFORT.

FINE.

HONEY? YOU OKAY?

GOOD, 'CAUSE YOU HAVE SOME GUESTS.

WHAT?

I... I THOUGHT IT WOULD JUST WEAR OFF.

CURSES DON'T WEAR OFF. WHERE'S THAT BOOK?

IT DOESN'T HAVE A SPELL TO REMOVE THE CURSE?

IF IT DID, I WOULDN'T BE STANDING HERE, GENIUS.

WELL, THERE'S GOTTA BE SOMETHING.

HEY, GIMME THAT BACK!

I KNOW A FEW CURSES MYSELF, PAL. BACK OFF.

BULL. YOU DON'T KNOW ANY CURSES.

SHE DOESN'T KNOW ANY CURSES.

WELL?

CHAPTER THREE

VANYA, THEY JUST TELL US THAT.

THERE'RE NO GOBLINS IN HERE.

YOU'VE NEVER BEEN THERE BEFORE. YOU'RE MAKING IT UP.

YOU'D BETTER HOPE I'M NOT.

MY MOM TOLD ME NEVER TO GO INTO THE WOODS.

SHE SAID THERE'S GOBLINS.

THAS RIGHT, LAD. NO ONE 'ERE BUT US CHICKENS!

QUIT MESSING AROUND, BUTTERWORM.

I NEED A FAVOR.

HAR HAR. SURE THING.

ALWAYS HAPPY TEH HELP WEE JUICY MORSELS...

>EHEM<

MORTALS.

I'M TAKING A TRIP TO *GOBLIN TOWN*. I NEED A *GUIDE*.

OOH. LUV TEH, BUT CAN'T.

WHY *NOT?*

I BEEN *BANISHED*. DISGRACE TEH THE *SPECIES*, THEY SAID.

BEEN *CAUGHT* TOO MANY TIMES BY THE LIKES O' *YOU*.

THERE'S EVEN A *CHAPTER* 'BOUT HOW TEH DO IT IN SOME BOOK O' *WITCHCRAFT*.

HMM.

TELL YEH *WHAT*, LASSIE. I'LL GET ME LITTLE *BROTHER*. 'E KNOWS THEM TUNNELS BACK'ARDS AND FORWARDS.

YOU DON'T MEAN—

OI!

BUTTERBUG!

HELP!
MORTALS!

SHUT UP!

HMMPH!

REMEMBER ME?

GHFFFGGH!

I RECALL YOU ONCE TELLING ME WHAT AN *IMPORTANT* GOBLIN YOU ARE.

I'M LOOKING FOR THE *ORCHARDS* OF THE *TWILIGHT KING.* I'M *SURE* YOU KNOW ALL ABOUT IT.

ULP!

COURTNEY PROMISED TO LET THE CAPTIVE GOBLIN GO IF HE COOPERATED.

WE ARE HERE

GOBLIN MARKET

ROUND CHAMBER

STAIRS TO LOWER CHAMBERS

DREADFULL DUCHESS'S MANOR HOUSE

STAIRS

SUNLESS SEA

CHASM

BRIDGE

ORCHARDS

TWILIGHT KING'S CASTLE

COUGH!

I SUPPOSE I'M NOT THE FIRST HUMAN YOU'VE COME ACROSS TODAY.

I'LL TELL YOU WHERE THEY WENT IF YOU RELEASE ME.

I DON'T THINK THAT'S HOW IT'S GOING TO GO, CREATURE.

WOW!

IT'S LIKE DISNEYLAND MEETS LORD OF THE RINGS!

VANYA!

JUST A *TASTE*, MILADY.

PLEASE—

ULP!

BUT BE *CAREFUL*. IT'S A *HEADY* DRAFT.

VANYA! WHERE'D YOU GO?

AH AH!

WHAT?

WHERE ARE YOU *TAKING* ME?

AH! AH!

BLAKE? VANYA?

OH MY.

TSK TSK. SOME GOBLINS HAVE ALL THE LUCK.

ERGH?

YOU KNOW *WHAT?* I CHANGED MY MIND.

THESE BRAINFARTS CAN TAKE A *FLYING LEAP* FOR ALL I CARE. IT'S NOT MY PROBLEM.

COME ON.

LET'S GO *HOME* AND MAKE SOME COCOA.

COURTNEY THOUGHT ABOUT UNCLE ALOYSIUS.

"THESE THINGS *HAPPEN*." HE'D SAY.

"*I SHOULDN'T WORRY ABOUT IT.*"

THEN SHE THOUGHT ABOUT HOW SHE HAD ONCE FELT WHEN SHE'D FOUND HERSELF TRAPPED IN GOBLIN TOWN WITH NO WAY OUT.

I REALLY *HATE* THOSE GUYS.

GRAH!

WHERE AM I?

IN *DEEP TROUBLE*, MORTAL!

OH NO!

OH YES!

AND LET ME *TELL YOU*, I'M GOING TO MAKE SURE YOU GO TO THE *CRUELEST, WICKEDEST* ELDER OUT THERE.

AND IF I *EVER* CATCH THAT LITTLE *FRIEND* OF YOURS, I'LL *PERSONALLY* FEED HER TO *RAWHEAD* AND *BLOODY BONES.*

THANKS, BUT I REALLY NEED TO FIND MY FRIENDS.

JUST *POINT* ME IN THE RIGHT DIRECTION.

AH! AH!

THANKS.

COURTNEY FIGURED BLAKE HAD BEEN HUMILIATED ENOUGH, AND DIDN'T THINK RUBBING IT IN WOULD HELP MATTERS.

HOW'D YOU *FIND* ME?

BUT IT WAS ALL SHE COULD DO TO KEEP THE SARCASM OUT OF HER VOICE.

IT HELPS TO HAVE AN INSIDE *MAN*.

GRAH!

HOW'D YOU DO THIS?

I CAME *PREPARED.* BURN A BUNDLE OF THE RIGHT HERBS, AND THEY GO *RIGHT* TO SLEEP.

BUT KEEP IT *DOWN*.

THIS PLACE IS HORRIBLE!

WHY DOESN'T THE COVEN DO SOMETHING ABOUT IT?

I'M HERE TO SEE THE DUCHESS.

UMM... SHE AROUND?

IS SHE FOR *REAL*?

DUNNO. GUESS WE'D BETTER *HOPE* SO.

GRAH!

WHAT DO YOU *THINK*?

THIS AIN'T MY SHOW ANYMORE. LET'S *FOLLOW* HIM.

COURTNEY WASN'T SURE WHAT KIND OF RECEPTION SHE'D GET FROM THE DREADFUL DUCHESS, BUT SHE DIDN'T HAVE MANY OPTIONS.

IT FELT A BIT LIKE ASKING A GRIZZLY BEAR FOR A BITE OF ITS MEAL.

WHAT ARE YOU *DOING* HERE?

I WAS JUST PASSING BY. I'D HAVE *CALLED* FIRST, BUT I DON'T HAVE YOUR DAYTIME NUMBER.

DARE YOU *PRESUME* TO BELIEVE ME YOUR *FRIEND*?

I ALLOWED YOU TO *ESCAPE* THIS LAND ONCE *BEFORE* BECAUSE OF MY GENEROUS *NATURE*. BUT YOUR KIND HAS TAKEN *FAR* TOO MUCH FROM ME AND MINE TO *EVER* BE FORGIVEN.

I AM *NOT* YOUR FRIEND.

S-SORRY...

YOU WERE THE *LAST* LIVING *SOUL* TO BE WITH MY *CHILD* BEFORE HE *DIED*.

I SUPPOSE SO.

TELL ME OF HIM.

"WHO TO?"

OH MY.

CHAPTER FOUR

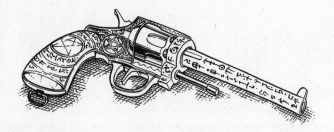

HMMMM....

Miss Crumrin & "friend"
Radley Hall 12-20

OH, EXCUSE ME, SIR. I WAS LOOKING FOR TEMPLETON.

MMM-HMM. I'VE BEEN LOOKING OVER THESE DOCUMENTS.

YOU KNOW, AS LUDICROUS AS IT SOUNDS, THIS EVIDENCE...

SIR?

BUT A YOUNG GIRL, DOING SUCH TERRIBLE THINGS ON HER OWN...

IT'S RIDICULOUS. UNLESS...

KEEPING AN EYE ON TEMPLETON, ARE YOU, COUNCILOR?

GIVEN HIS ATTITUDE ABOUT MY STUDENT, IT'D BE UNWISE NOT TO.

DO YOU KNOW WHERE HE MIGHT BE?

NO, AS A MATTER OF FACT, I DON'T...

MMM, I'M HUNGRY...

EAT, SISTER. THERE IS PLENTY.

LET ME POUR YOU SOME WINE.

NO, I'M NOT SUPPOSED TO!

COME BACK, SISTER.

WE WON'T HARM YOU.

AS COURTNEY GAZED UPON THE VAST FORTRESS, HER RESOLVE DEFLATED LIKE A WEEK-OLD BALLOON.

OH, BUGGER.

SHE KNEW SHE WAS POWERLESS AGAINST THIS ADVERSARY. HER BAG OF TRICKS HAD RUN OUT. THE OTHERS HUNG THEIR HEADS, AS THOUGH ALREADY DEFEATED.

BUT THE THOUGHT OF SIMPLY SLINKING AWAY WAS TOO BITTER.

THEY HAD ALL PASSED THE POINT OF NO RETURN, AND THE ONLY WAY OUT OF THE MESS THEY'D CREATED WAS FORWARD...

...TO WHATEVER FATE LAY AT THE ROAD'S END.

WON'T YOU SIT DOWN?

WHO ARE YOU?

DO YOU NOT KNOW ME, CONSTANCE?

I HAVE KNOWN YOU ALL YOUR LIFE. I'VE WATCHED YOU FROM AFAR.

YOU'VE BEEN SPYING ON ME?

NO, MY DEAR. YOU SPIED ON ME.

EACH TIME YOU PEERED FROM THE WINDOW OF YOUR NURSERY...

...AND LONGED TO EXPLORE THE WILD, MAGICAL REALM BEYOND...

... YOU WERE CALLING MY NAME.

WE FLED, BUT MY QUEEN WOULD NOT FLEE WITH US.

SHE VOWED TO STAY IN THE DWINDLING WILDS OF THE EARTH UNTIL THEY WERE NO MORE.

I'VE SEARCHED, BUT I CAN NO LONGER FIND HER.

ALL I HAVE LEFT ARE MY DAUGHTERS, THOUGH SOME HAVE SCORNED ME, WHILE OTHERS GO IN SEARCH OF THEIR MOTHER, NEVER TO RETURN.

I CAN BEAR EXILE, BUT TO BE ALONE IN THIS SHADOW REALM...

STAY WITH US, CONSTANCE.

YOU WOULD HAVE THREE DEVOTED SISTERS FOR COMPANY, AND LIVE FOREVER AWAY FROM MORTAL SORROWS...

AND I WOULD LOVE YOU AS MY OWN DAUGHTER.

PLEASE, WON'T YOU STAY?

THE DISTANCE PLAYED TRICKS. THE GATE APPEARED VAST FROM AFAR, AND YET SEEMED TO GROW BEYOND MEASURE AS THEY APPROACHED.

IT WAS THE LONGEST ROAD COURTNEY HAD EVER TROD.

STOP!

WHAT THE DEVIL ARE YOU DOING?

IS *THAT* WHAT SHE TOLD YOU?

WHAT?

OUR *FRIEND* IS IN THERE! WE'RE TRYING TO *RESCUE* HER.

LOOK WHERE YOU'RE *GOING!* THIS *FRIEND* OF YOURS IS LEADING YOU ALL TO *HELL!*

WHO *IS* THIS GUY?

I'M THE LAW, GIRL.

AND YOU'RE UNDER ARREST.

PUT THESE ON.

PUT—GIMME A BREAK!

THE REST OF YOU, GET BEHIND ME. WE'RE GETTING OUT OF HERE.

WHAT ABOUT OUR FRIEND?

CONNIE'S STILL IN THERE.

LISTEN TO ME! I DON'T KNOW WHAT LIES THIS GIRL HAS BEEN SPEWING, BUT NOTHING IS GOING TO CONVINCE ME TO LET YOU WALK THROUGH THAT DOOR.

ALL RIGHT, DUDE, CALM DOWN.

GUYS, JUST BACK AWAY FROM THE CRAZY MAN.

>COUGH<
>COUGH<

WHAT A SUCKY WEEK.

WHERE'S THE BIG CREEPY SUPER-WARLOCK UNCLE WHEN YOU NEED ONE?

WELL, WELL. LOOK WHO IT IS. LITTLE COURTNEY CRUMRIN.

WHO'S THERE?

DON'T YOU RECOGNIZE ME?

AFTER ALL, IT WAS YOU WHO CONDEMNED ME TO THIS PLACE.

HECTOR.

I KNEW YOU'D EVENTUALLY END UP HERE TOO...

...THOUGH I WASN'T EXPECTING YOU SO SOON.

WHERE ARE WE?

DON'T YOU KNOW?

THIS IS TOMMY RAWHEAD'S LAIR. ALL WICKED LITTLE BOYS AND GIRLS END UP HERE.

I'VE DREAMED OF THIS MOMENT, LET ME TELL YOU.

TO WATCH OL' TOMMY GOBBLE YOU UP AND SPIT OUT YOUR NAKED BONES.

SUCH THOUGHTS KEPT ME WARM IN THIS COLD PLACE.

WAKE UP, TOMMY.

DID SOMEONE MENTION MY NAME?

YOU HAVE A GUEST.

HA HA! DON'T GO. EVEN HELL ISN'T SO BAD WHEN YOU HAVE COMPANY.

YOU REALLY ARE JUST CRAP, AREN'T YOU?

BECAUSE I WANT VENGEANCE?

I'M THE WOUNDED PARTY, MISSY. WHAT HAD I EVER DONE TO YOU?

YOU KNOW WHAT YOU DID.

AS DO YOU, GIRL.

AS DO YOU.

HUH?

MARSHAL? IS THAT YOU?

WHERE ARE YOU?

WHO'S THERE?

TEMPLETON!

HERE.

OH, LORD. HOW...

WHAT HAPPENED TO YOU?

CRUMRIN'S GRAND-NIECE.

SHE'S A DEVIL-CHILD.

I KNEW IT!

WHAT ABOUT THE PROFESSOR? AND CRISP? DID THEY KNOW?

YES, THEY ALL KNEW. IT WAS A CONSPIRACY.

ALOYSIUS! HE WANTS TO RULE THE COVEN.

NO!

Thunk!

HHHHSSSSSSSSS

KEEP GOING!

I'M RISKING MY NECK TO SAVE YOURS, KID.

GET MOVING, OR I'LL SHOOT YOU MYSELF.

GRAH!!!

NO YOU WON'T.

RRRRAAAAAWWWWWWWRRRR!!!!

C'MON!

BUT...

WE STILL HAVE A JOB TO DO.

OH. YES.

k-kl

GRRRRRLLLLL!

BLAM!

MONSTERS.

EAT SILVER, YOU HORROR.

MORTAL!

COURTNEY WAS RIGHT. THE CHILDREN, THOUGH EXHAUSTED TO THE POINT OF COLLAPSE, DID STILL HAVE A PRESSING ERRAND.

WHERE IS HE?

GRAH.

JOEY?

IS THAT YOU?

WE'VE COME TO TAKE YOU HOME. REMEMBER?

WAIT! DON'T GO.

JOEY, PLEASE, COME HOME. MOM AND DAD'LL FREAK OUT.

I KNOW THIS IS ALL MY FAULT AND I'M SORRY...

BUT IF YOU COME HOME, I PROMISE I'LL...

YOU'RE...

UNDER...

ARREST!

WHAT IS IT WITH YOU *MARSHALS*? DID THE AD SAY "TWISTED NUT-JOBS ONLY"?

WHAT'D I DO TO *YOU*?

WHAT DID YOU-!?!

MURDERED MARSHAL *HUGHES!* DID YOUR BEST TO LEAD THOSE KIDS TO THE DEVIL HIMSELF.

YOU... YOU'RE A *FIEND!*

CALM DOWN, MISTER.

CALM DOWN!?! I OUGHT TO KILL YOU HERE AND *NOW!* YOU'RE A WALKING *MENACE.*

YOU DON'T KNOW WHAT YOU'RE TALKING ABOUT.

COURTNEY SAVED ALL OUR LIVES.

COURTNEY THOUGHT SHE'D KNOWN EXHAUSTION, BUT THE WAY SHE FELT NOW WAS UNREAL.

SHE WAS TOO TIRED EVEN TO NOTICE THE FIGURE THAT STOOD WAITING IN THE DARKNESS JUST OUTSIDE THE WARM GLOW OF HOME.

COURTNEY AWOKE THE NEXT MORNING FEELING LIKE A WADDED UP PIECE OF PAPER. THE DAY WAS OFF TO A BAD START BEFORE SHE EVEN OPENED HER EYES.

HAPPY *BIRTHDAY,* HONEY.

...GRUMBLE...

PRESENTS TURNED OUT TO BE A COMPLETE SET OF GLORIA VANDERBILT MAKEUP, A "RAZOR EXTREME!" ELECTRIC SCOOTER, AND THE COUP DE GRACE...

BRACES?

YOU'LL HAVE *PERFECT* TEETH. MAYBE YOU'LL EVEN WANT TO *SMILE* MORE.

YOU WANT THEM, *DON'T* YOU? ALL THE KIDS WANT BRACES...

SURE, DAD. THANKS.

GOOD MORNING.

AM I TOO LATE FOR *CAKE?*

OH, HEY, UNCLE A. WHAT'S UP?

I JUST THOUGHT I'D DROP IN AND GIVE YOU YOUR PRESENT.

WHAT'S THIS? PLANE TICKETS?

WHERE'S, UH, PRAAGEW?

MS. CRISP SUGGESTED THAT YOU MIGHT WANT TO JOIN ME ON MY TRAVELS THIS SUMMER.

AND I CERTAINLY WOULD BE HAPPY TO HAVE YOU.

IF YOU'RE INTERESTED, OF COURSE.

HMMM. SOUND'S PRETTY COOL.

I'LL THINK ABOUT IT.

WELL THAT'S THEM TWO PATCHED UP.

DON'T IT MAKE YEH WANT TEH PUKE?

YEH THINK THAT'S BAD, I WON'T EVEN TELL YEH WHAT HAPPENED THE NEXT DAY AT SCHOOL.

IT'S JUST TOO 'ORRIBLE TO CONTEMPLATE.

HAPPY ✶ BIRTHDAY ✶ CORTNEY

DON'T LOOK AT ME. I WAS AGAINST THE WHOLE THING.

SURPRISE!

HAPPY BIRTHDAY.

Happy Birthday Courtney

WHAT THE HECK IS THIS?

IT'S CALLED 'FRIENDSHIP'. YOU'LL GET USED TO IT.

GREAT. LIKE I DON'T HAVE ENOUGH PAIN.

PULL ANOTHER STUNT LIKE YESTERDAY AND YOU'LL FIND OUT WHAT REAL PAIN IS.

Among readers of the spookier sorts of comics, Ted Naifeh is a fan favorite. Since the early nineties, he's done illustration work for a wide variety of publishers, ranging from Marvel to Dark Horse to Wizards of the Coast. *Courtney Crumrin* represents his first published writing, and has been surprisingly well received. The original mini-series, *Courtney Crumrin and the Night Things*, was nominated for an Eisner award for best limited series in 2003.

Ted is also the co-creator of works such as the goth romance *GloomCookie* and the groundbreaking *How Loathsome*, now collected at NBM. He is currently starting work on his next project with Oni Press, the multi-volume fantasy epic *Glimmer*.

Ted resides in San Francisco because he loves fog.